Appliqué 12 Borders & Medallions!

by Elly Sienkiewicz

PATTERNS FROM EASY TO HEIRLOOM

A PATTERN COMPANION TO VOLUME III
OF BALTIMORE BEAUTIES & BEYOND

 C&T PUBLISHING

©1994 Eleanor Patton Hamilton Sienkiewicz

All photographs not otherwise credited are by the author

Electronic pattern illustrations by Gretchen N. Schwarzenbach

Cloth prints from the 1993 *Elly Sienkiewicz Baltimore Beauties* for P & B Textiles'
Designer Collection fill many of the shapes in the pattern section.

Front cover photograph by Jack Mathieson, Woodland Hills, California
Cover designed by Judy Benjamin

Editing by Louise Owens Townsend
Technical editing by Joyce Engels Lytle

Design and production coordination by Judy Benjamin, *Meridian*
P.O. Box 1887, Orinda, California 94563

Published by C&T Publishing, P.O. Box 1456, Lafayette, California 94549

ISBN 0-914881-76-0 (Hardcover)
ISBN 0-914881-80-9 (Softcover)

Library of Congress Cataloging-in-Publication Data

Sienkiewicz, Elly.
    Appliqué 12 borders and medallions!: patterns from easy to
heirloom / by Elly Sienkiewicz. — 1st ed.
      p.   cm.
    "A Pattern companion to volume III of Baltimore beauties and
beyond, studies in classic Baltimore album quilts."
     ISBN 0-914881-76-0 (hdbk.) — ISBN 0-914881-80-9 (pbk.)
     1. Appliqué—Patterns. 2. Album quilts—Maryland—Baltimore.
3. Patchwork—Patterns. 4. Borders, Ornamental (Decorative arts)
5. Medallions (Decorative arts) I. Sienkiewicz, Elly. Baltimore
beauties and beyond. II. Title. III. Title: Appliqué twelve borders
and medallions!
TT779.S528 1994
746.44'5041—dc20   94-2012
                     CIP

Printed in the United States
First Edition

10   9   8   7   6   5   4   3   2   1

Acknowledgments

*T*his book brings the *Baltimore Beauties®* series to within one book of its conclusion. My special thanks to my publishers, Todd and Tony Hensley, for their faith in the *Baltimore Beauties* series and in this book, and for being publishers I am both proud and fond of. And to C&T Publishing's talented production team: Editorial Design Director, Diane Pedersen; Editor, Louise Townsend; and Technical Editor, Joyce Lytle. On the homefront, this series has entailed a major orchestration of many individuals and institutions. Multiple threads have had to be kept untangled through the years of its writing. This organizational endeavor's success is due in large part to the gracious assistance of Denise Scott. Her talents are so diverse and her virtues so many, that I am forever grateful that we are associates. Thank you, Denise! And to my family, special thanks to my husband, Stan, and my daughter, Katya (our last child still at home), who pitch in cheerfully and enable me to enjoy school sports, sit-down suppers, folded laundry—and their very special presence.

The borders and medallions herein are based on antique Album Quilts. Drafted from photos, some changed a bit in the drawing, as the spirit moved me. So inevitably, they have been brought a bit "beyond" Baltimore. One, "Bonnie's Hearts and Angels Border," is my neighbor, Kathryn Blomgren Campbell's original design. But even where I have drafted the pattern and provided the cloth, the needleartists put a wealth of creative interpretation into the materialization of these borders and medallions. Without the needleartists, this series could never have been. Some, particularly those who stitched on the Classic Revival Album (1985-1991), gave their gift so long ago, and now it will shine at series' end in *Volume III*. There, all of its block patterns will be given in full, and all of its needleartists' brief biographies will appear. Thank you, each and every one.

Most of the border and medallion patterns pictured in the Color Section of this book are on contemporary quilts. For this rebirth, my heartfelt thanks and appreciation go to:

Kathryn Blomgren Campbell, Nonna Crook, Barbara Hahl, Ruth Meyers, Joy Nichols, Sylvia Pickell, Yolanda Tovar, Albertine Veenstra; makers of the Classic Revival Album (listed in *Volume III*); and the friends of Mary Sue Thomas Hannan (listed in *Volume I*) who stitched "Friendship's Offering" for her 70th birthday. And now, Happy 77th, Sue!

❀ ❀ ❀

Dedication

To Teachers of Baltimore Beauties, everywhere—

Your skilled sharing makes forgotten techniques commonplace once again. Yet you nourish uncommon quilts—legacies—the future's classics. You help other quiltmakers by the practical, the personal, and the pep talk. And so, in admiration, I dedicate this source book to each of you. It contains both easy borders and ambitious borders, and two medallions: one a dramatic, but simpler medallion, and one, which became, in the makers' hands, a masterpiece of dimensional flowers and embroidery. Each pattern is perfect for someone, for someone's turn-of-the-20th-century Album Quilt. With your help, they'll find it here and make it their own. This is to you, for the inspiration and help you give us all, with my thanks and appreciation.

Table of Contents

The Home-Grown Rose Border

• Design Source: From a mid-19th-century Album Quilt pictured in *The Central New Jersey Home News,* on Saturday, September 13, 1986.

• Diagram of the full border: page 15

• Width of Finished Border: 8¾" deep (including a Dogtooth Triangle edging border)

• Length of the Border Repeat: 5½" repeat

• Appliqué Ease Level: Easy

• Methods from *Appliqué 12 Easy Ways:* Triangles, Stems, #1 and #2; Buds, Blossoms, #8. See Dogtooth Border Workshop, *Volume II,* page 78.

Bonnie's Hearts and Angels Border

• Design Source: From Bonnie's Album (Quilt #7 in the Color Section) a contemporary Album Quilt designed and made by Kathryn Blomgren Campbell.

• Diagram of the full border: page 16

• Width of Finished Border: 12½" deep (including a Dogtooth Triangle edging border)

• Length of the Border Repeat: 7¼" repeat

• Appliqué Ease Level: Hearts and Swags, Super Easy! Angels, A Challenge

• Methods from *Appliqué 12 Easy Ways:* Swags, #2; Hearts and Angels, #4 and #8

The Rose of Sharon Border

• Design Source: From an antebellum Baltimore-style quilt, the heavily stuffed and embroidered Album (Quilt #6 in the Color Section.)

• Diagram of the full border: page 20

• Width of Finished Border: 8" deep

• Length of the Border Repeat: 10⅛" repeat

• Appliqué Ease Level: A Challenge

• Methods from *Appliqué 12 Easy Ways:* #2, #4, and #8

The Mirrored-Ribbon Border

• Design Source: From a 19th-century Album, Quilt #2 in *Design a Baltimore Album Quilt.* (A version of this border is pictured on Quilt #9 in the Color Section.)

• Diagram of the full border: page 23

• Width of Finished Border: 13" deep

• Length of the Border Repeat: 17" repeat

• Appliqué Ease Level: Super Easy!

• Methods from *Appliqué 12 Easy Ways:* #1, #2, and #8

Tasseled-Ribbon Swag Border

- Design Source: From a mid-19th-century Album.
- Diagram of the full border: page 26
- Width of Finished Border: 9" deep
- Length of the Border Repeat: 6½" repeat
- Appliqué Ease Level: Super Easy!
- Methods from *Appliqué 12 Easy Ways*: #1, #2, and #8

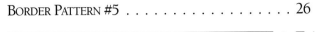

Beribboned Feather Border

- Design Source: From Quilt #8 in *Volume II*, a classic Baltimore Album Quilt whose inscriptions include "Baltimore" and "1850." This border is pictured on a contemporary quilt, Quilt #2 in the Color Section.
- Diagram of the full border: page 28
- Width of Finished Border: 11" deep
- Length of the Side Border Repeat: 77½" repeat
- Length of the Top Border Repeat: 38¾" repeat
- Length of the Bottom Border Repeat: 38¾" repeat
- Appliqué Ease Level: A Challenge
- Method from *Appliqué 12 Easy Ways*: #3

The Dancing Grapevine Border

- Design Source: Original design by the author. This border is pictured on a group quilt, Quilt #4 in the Color Section, where it is framed by a Stepped Border (three steps), based on Pattern #32 in *Volume II*.
- Diagram of the full border: page 61

- Width of Finished Border: 12" deep (including an edging border)
- Length of the Border Repeat: 24¼" repeat
- Appliqué Ease Level: A Challenge
- Methods from *Appliqué 12 Easy Ways*: #4, #11, and #12

The Palmetto-Tied Laurel Garland Border

- Design Source: From the Classic Revival Album, Quilt #5 in the Color Section. (Contemporary group quilt designed by the author and based on the Sarah Seidenstricker Baltimore Album Quilt. 1845 is appliquéd on that quilt's border.)
- Diagram of the full border: page 70
- Width of Finished Border: 12" deep
- Length of the Border Repeat: 45" repeat
- Appliqué Ease Level: A Challenge
- Methods from *Appliqué 12 Easy Ways*: #4, #11, and #12; Palmetto, #2

Friendship's Offering Border

- Design Source: Based on an 1847 Pennsylvania quilt by Sarah Holcombe. This border is pictured on Quilt #8 in the Color Section, where it is framed by an edging border, Pattern #30 in *Volume II*.
- Diagram of the full border: page 75
- Width of Finished Border: 11" deep
- Length of the Side Border Repeat: 3¼" repeat
- Length of the Top Border Repeat: 6½" repeat
- Length of the Bottom Border Repeat: 5⅜" repeat
- Appliqué Ease Level: A Challenge
- Methods from *Appliqué 12 Easy Ways*: #2, #4, and #11

BORDER PATTERN #10 . . . . PULLOUT

The Straight Rose-Vine Border

• Design Source: From a mid-19th-century Baltimore-style Album, Quilt #1 in *Design a Baltimore Album Quilt*. This border is pictured on Quilt #3 in the Color Section.

• Diagram of the full border: on the pull-out sheet

• Width of Finished Border: 8⅛" deep

• Length of the Border Repeat: 10¼" repeat

• Appliqué Ease Level: Easy

• Methods from *Appliqué 12 Easy Ways*: #4, # 8, and #11

MEDALLION PATTERN #11 . . . . PULLOUT

Bowl of Flowers in a Rose Wreath

• Design Source: From a mid-19th-century Baltimore-style Album, Quilt #1 in *Design a Baltimore Album Quilt*. This medallion is pictured on Quilt #3 in the Color Section.

• Diagram of the full medallion: on the pull-out sheet

• Size of Design Image: The medallion is based on four 12½" blocks (25" square) but more background space can be left, depending on the size needed for your set.

• Appliqué Ease Level: Moderately Easy

• Methods from *Appliqué 12 Easy Ways*: #8, #11, and #12

MEDALLION PATTERN #12 . . . . PULLOUT

Feather-Wreathed Album in a Rose Lyre

• Design Source: This combines an 1850 Baltimore medallion center (Quilt #8 in *Volume II*) with a block enlarged from a second antique Baltimore Album Quilt. See this medallion on Quilt #2 in the Color Section.

• Diagram of the full medallion: on the pull-out sheet

• Size of Design Image: The medallion is based on four 12½" blocks (25" square) but more background space can be left, depending on the size needed for your set.

• Appliqué Ease Level: A Challenge

• Methods from *Appliqué 12 Easy Ways*: #3, #4, and #11

The Color Section begins after page 32.

Introduction

*W*hy are there just three volumes, but now eight books (and a ninth on the way) in the *Baltimore Beauties* series? The short answer is that it is both an idea that grew like topsy, and it is my great good fortune to have a publisher willing to support my wide-ranging exploration in this fascinating quilt genre.

We met in the hotel coffee shop after the Merchant Mall take-down. Carolie and Tom Hensley had brought "The Cotton Patch," Carolie's quilt shop, to vend at the West Coast Quilters' Conference. That was July 1988. DeLoris and Herb Stude ran the conference then, and Carolie and Tom had begun a quilt book publishing venture five years earlier. In the down-to-earth style for which they became known, they had named it C&T for Carolie and Tom. Years later, Tom asked what I thought about changing that business name. "It has history," I replied. "And you could grow in any direction with it. People don't really know what C&T stands for. It could be quite sophisticated—or not. And it's already got such a good reputation. I like it." But that night, when we three met for the first time, we were all tired.

I had posted query letters to ten publishers, peddling my proposed how-to-make-a-Baltimore-Album-Quilt book. Having already self-published a pattern book/symbol dictionary (*Spoken Without a Word,* 1983) on these quilts, my letter explained, I felt we were ready for some "how-to lessons" on the subject and color pictures. Tom wrote that C&T was indeed interested in publishing such a book. So we arranged to meet over coffee. Other than the fact that we were all quite exhausted from working the conference, I just remember shaking hands on getting a manuscript in by April 1989.

That January, I phoned Tom in California. "You said no more than 96 pages, and I already have more than 150 pages, just of block patterns," I reported anxiously. We talked the problem through. *Baltimore Beauties* should be a three-volume series, we decided, not just a single book. The first volume would be a how-to-appliqué-the-blocks book. Thus, *Baltimore Beauties and Beyond, Studies in*

Classic Album Quilt Appliqué, Volume I was born in September 1989. It was a chunky birthling at 176 pages. Tom wrote tersely that he was "not happy about that." Nonetheless, *Volume I* became quite popular. It added dramatically to my own teaching schedule and set off Baltimore-style Album Quilt classes and Album Quilt stitch-study circles across the country.

That January of 1989, when we had changed *Volume I's* target, I worried over the phone to Doris Seeley, who was arranging for me to teach in Colorado. "I can write the book or make the models, but not both," I lamented. Though we had never met, Doris offered to ask if any in her appliqué group might be willing to help. They became the first of the needleartists, who, one-by-one, stitch-by-stitch, helpful-hand-by-helpful-hand, were part of the team that brought the *Baltimore Beauties* series to life. They stitched many of the lesson kits, and their names are among those mentioned in gratitude throughout this nine-book series. One kind benefactress explained that her husband wondered why she would contribute her time and talent to *Baltimore Beauties*. She told him that she enjoyed the series a great deal, but knew that one person could not do it alone. She felt it had enriched her life and wanted to help make it into something greater still. Such friendship and generosity is gratifying, and the honor comes sometimes even from people I have yet to meet.

By the time *Volume I* had been published, interest in these quilts had broadened and deepened. "These quilts are just fascinating," readers would say. "I'd love to know more about their history." So a *Pattern Companion,* aimed at this fascination (and slipped into the series between *Volumes I* and *II*) was proposed to C&T. It would consist of block patterns with photos of the antique originals annotated with the history each reflected. When *Baltimore Album Quilts, Historic Notes and Antique Patterns* weighed in at 56 patterns and 184 pages, Tom was not sure it should be published. "We're in the business of publishing quilt books, not history books," he noted dryly. His son, Todd, in the process of taking over the publishing house administration, telephoned me to suggest that maybe this manuscript should be considered *Volume II* and the next one *Volume III;* and then we'd all call it quits.

Over a fine seafood dinner, as Tom and Carolie's guest, I argued for that book's publication. Tom examined the pros and cons right through the main course. But by dessert, he said firmly, "We'll do it." Then he added, "but we'll have to change the title." He has a genius for titles and authored one consistent with the book's contents. Dinner ended happily. I promised the book would sell. And, thank heaven, sell it did. "Baltimores," which so many had dismissed as "too hard," were catching on.

By the winter of 1989, my involvement in these quilts had led me into a bit of historical detective work. The art and antique world's growing attribution of numbers of Baltimore-style Album Quilts solely to Mary Evans had come to seem ill-founded to me. I researched that issue and incorporated my findings into *Volume II.* In the production of *Volume II,* we had to overcome design problems, but its written text remains my favorite. Two beautiful poems by Margaret Fleisher Kaufman set the mood. The nature of Victorian Albums is discussed; calligraphy, inked embellishment, and the making of picture blocks are taught. Then a photo-tour of 50 Album Quilts introduces the idiosyncrasies of Album-set style. It is *Volume II* that presents the first 13 border patterns, along with 20 more block patterns. But readers wrote that they wanted more discussion about borders. And more border patterns. And more block patterns.

Volume I's reception was both heartwarming, and surprising. Not only were Baltimore Albums masterpieces, bringing huge sums in the antique world; but, judged from the block production the book seemed to inspire, you and I could aspire to make one. Hand appliqué, ran its message, is a pleasing, easily learned skill with a multitude of delightful approaches—literally, something for everyone. Once that news was out, it was *Volume I's* folded and gathered flowers that, above all else, seemed to catch quiltmakers' imaginations. From then on, it was clear that the series would have to include a book on how to make dimensional flowers. Soon, the techniques amassed were voluminous. One couldn't do justice to manipulated floral appliqué, I explained to Todd, unless the "quilt design material" scheduled for the next book were pulled away from the flowers and put in a separate book of its own. Happily, Todd and Tony (Carolie and Tom's sons, now owners of the publishing house) agreed to its addition. So in 1992, *Design a Baltimore Album Quilt! A Teach Yourself Course in Sets and Borders,* the fourth in the series, became the *Design Companion to Volume II.* That book was also the first in the series to include all of the block and border patterns needed to reproduce a complete antique Album,

The Heart-Garlanded Album.

Quiltmakers were ready for a book on "fancy flowers." Actually, they had been since *Volume I.* I'd written numerous articles, but not the book. In fact, I couldn't seem to write that book. Either I had "writer's block" or I couldn't stop making those endearing flowers, or both. *Dimensional Appliqué, The Pattern Companion to Volume II* was the hardest book for me to settle down to write in the entire series. Then, with something akin to relief, I patterned its approach on *Volume I's* lesson format, and the book was published. Dimensional flowers had already seeded themselves throughout the quilt world. They were being cultivated in every conceivable kind of quilt. And, quite suddenly it seemed, the Baltimore-style Albums being made by quilters were coming at last into completion. They had a distinctive turn-of-the-20th-century vitality all their own. By the last decade of our century, quiltmakers had quite clearly taken Baltimore "beyond"!

As the series grew, it, too, was taking on a fresher look, thanks in large part to the guidance of Editorial Design Director, Diane Pedersen. All told, it seemed the heyday of appliqué and of Albums, once again. In recognition, P & B Textiles printed a wonderful "Baltimore Beauties" line of fabric in 1993 and augmented more prints in 1994. And C&T, the series' patron as well as publisher, honored all appliqué Album Quilt makers with a gala contest, show, and celebration. Dubbed "Baltimore Revival!" it was held in Lancaster, Pennsylvania, in April 1994. Coincident with that happening, the show catalog, *Baltimore Album Revival! Historic Quilts in the Making,* the series' seventh book, debuted. A colorful synopsis of these remarkable Baltimore-style Revivalist Album Quilts, the catalog documents the state of their art. An intriguing essay explores why making these painstaking quilts has such broad contemporary appeal. And its answers may surprise you.

Finally, gala finale in sight, *Volume III* was underway. Would the series be completed at last, by the time of the big show? With a sudden realization, the answer was "No." More had been promised than could actually be delivered in this last "volume." The most elaborate borders and medallions, for example, had been saved for last. More than 80 pages of these long-proffered patterns left insufficient room for the planned conclusion: silhouette and paper-cut design lessons; fruit portrayal with "gauging" (a decorative gathering to size) and stencil-shading; a plethora of paper-cut block patterns; and then summation of the whole remarkable Baltimore phenomenon. But could there be another book?

C&T's Editorial Board convened to assess how best to deliver *Baltimore Beauties,* now a series with its own story, through to conclusion. *Appliqué 12 Borders and Medallions!* has solved the problem, and, given space of its own, presents the borders and medallions in a relaxed and easy-to-follow format. (Regrettably, Dear Reader, as the series has grown, index references in earlier volumes have sometimes become misplaced. Please understand.) With this book in hand, the series' conclusion fell smoothly into place. The one original Baltimore book had mushroomed, and also had become, in the process, something of a modern Album Quilt time capsule. With *Volume III,* that capsule could finally be sealed. Felicitously, recently unearthed documents cleared up many of the questions surrounding Baltimore's Albums so that *Volume III* provides both the series' lessons and its historical themes with a happy ending. As for its publisher, C&T's faith in this eight- (and about to become nine-) book cycle, though tested, has held steady, and is very much appreciated.

And now you know the answer to how one book grew into three, and how three volumes had more than doubled in number before *Volume III* had even been pub-lished. But what pleasure their writing has brought me; what admiration I have, still, for these fascinating ladies of bygone Baltimore. And how it has comforted me to know that so many of you have found them similarly compelling. Do we understand these old quilts and their makers? A bit, I think. But an air of mystery nonetheless enfolds them. And so they hold me, still.

None of this, not *Spoken Without a Word,* not *Volumes I* and more, not this flower-filled revival of heirloom proportions, could ever have happened without you who read this, now. You have stitched along with this series on a joyful odyssey from Baltimore to "beautifully beyond." You have read the books and made the blocks and sewn the quilts; then shared notecards, thoughts, and snapshots. I have enjoyed the journey so. Thank you for your company, for your friendship.

Elly Sienkiewicz
September 17, 1993

Part One: Getting Started

*B*ordering a quilt is a bit like wrapping a gift. When you make an added effort in its presentation, the viewer sees instantly that the contents are valued, special. Appliqué borders can be simple or intricate, and they can frame pieced quilts as well as appliquéd ones. Appliqué borders have a special cachet. Through the centuries they've been recognized as an elegant finish, a significant additional investment on the quiltmaker's part. In the past decade or so, we have learned, or re-discovered, such wonderful ways to make appliqué easier, more pleasant, less time-consuming, by hand as well as by machine. For many of us, this newly discovered skill makes including appliqué borders on our own quilts ever so much more inviting. Let's look at how this book is organized, then at how its patterns are presented, so that each and every one of them will be as close as your fingertips.

The Table of Contents carries important notes about each pattern, as well as an initial illustration of that pattern. In addition to giving the design source, it assesses the ease with which a given pattern can be executed—Super Easy! Easy, Moderately Easy, and A Challenge. And, although this is a pattern book only, a reference for the method I personally would use to stitch each pattern is given. Most refer to my simplest how-to book, *Appliqué 12 Easy Ways!* But where more specialized techniques are required, books from my *Baltimore Beauties and Beyond* series are cited. While all of these books concentrate on hand appliqué, they include a few words on machine appliqué where substituting a bit of simple machine work makes the handwork even easier. *Note:* Often appliqué motifs on the border are larger than those within the body of the quilt. This easier scale gives you the choice of doing some or all of the appliqué by machine as well as by hand. At this stage in my life, I personally prefer hand appliqué. But, for sewing the initial seam of a "superfine stem" down on a border or on a medallion wreath, for example, I would sew that simple running stitch on my machine. Sew these patterns as you choose. There is no one way to do it. Your way is the best way!

How to Use the Patterns in this Book

Complete, fully drawn and laid-out patterns for 10 borders and two medallions are given in this book. The book's pattern format is simple and straight-forward: One corner is given, then one repeat of the adjacent border. A repeat is that unit, which repeated (either right-side up, flopped over, or else alternating first one way, then the other), makes up the desired length of the border between the border corners. The repeat is bracketed by dashed lines noted on the pattern and the length of the repeat is given.

A header at the top of each pattern page gives the pattern's name and number, then tells how many pages long the pattern is, and from which side (left or right) of the corner the pattern is being presented. The borders are sized to the original quilt in which they appear. Certain center-running borders are framed by edging borders in the original. When those edging borders were already given in *Baltimore Beauties and Beyond, Volume II*, they aren't repeated here. The patterns' stated width includes room for those edgings, however.

WILL YOU HAVE TO TAILOR THE BORDERS TO FIT YOUR PARTICULAR QUILT?

Almost certainly yes, because the block sizes in the original quilts vary (from 12½" to 18" finished), and some are set with sashing, some are not. To walk you through this sizing process, excellent guidance in making a Master Border Pattern and in tailoring your border is given in *Design a Baltimore Album Quilt!* (pages 66 to 72).

Most of the borders in this book have one short repeat and are both easy to transfer and easy to adjust in length to your quilt's needs. Three of the borders (Patterns #6, 7, and 8) however, have long repeats and are tailored to specific block sets. These patterns consume a great many pattern pages, but the pattern transfer process is the same for these as for the patterns which are presented on only two to three pages.

Transferring a Border Pattern

1. Cut a "master pattern"

The master pattern is a piece of paper the size and shape of the finished border. It is your layout pattern for the individual appliqués that make up the border design. Cut your master pattern out of freezer paper or large sheets of graph paper. Cut it to the finished width and half the finished length of the border. For most quilts, a master pattern that is half the length of the finished border is sufficient. If the design moves in the same direction around the border you can simply move the half-border pattern on to the second half of the border. If the second half mirrors the first half, you can trace the second half to the back of the master border pattern, using a light box. In *Appliqué 12 Borders and Medallions!* there is one exception: the side border of Pattern #6. For ease, it needs a master pattern the full length of the border.

2. Trace or photocopy each pattern page onto an 8½" x 11" sheet of paper

Include the border's inner seam line and the horizontal page frame lines on each copy. These lines act as your registration marks to ensure that the pattern stays positioned properly when you transfer it. The easiest thing to do is to tape photocopies onto a master border pattern (rather than trace them) in the proper sequence. Use repositionable tape to make this process easier.

3. Transferring the copied patterns to the master pattern

Repeat the units according to the instructions on the printed pattern to form one long master pattern. *Note:* The finished width of the border is the portion that shows between the inner seam and the outer quilt binding. Read *Design a Baltimore Album Quilt!* (page 72) about adding adjustment allowances when you cut the actual border background cloth.

BORDER CORNERS

All of the patterns in this book are accompanied by border corners. Sometimes these attach to running borders. Sometimes, even when the border itself is a running border, the corners are separate. These separate-unit corners may vary one from another, just as in some quilts, the borders vary from one side of the quilt to another. Whichever the case, each border pattern includes its corner patterns here.

MARKING, APPLIQUÉING AND FINISHING

Appliqué 12 Easy Ways!, *Baltimore Beauties and Beyond, Volumes I* and *II*, and *Dimensional Appliqué* have useful technical information on the appliqué process. The method you use to appliqué the border determines how you mark the border. For example, with cut-away appliqué you mark the appliqué fabric. With freezer paper inside, you may do minimal marking on the background cloth itself. Decide on your appliqué method before making any marks on the background cloth.

WHERE CAN I FIND QUILT BLOCK PATTERNS TO MAKE THE QUILTS PICTURED IN THE COLOR SECTION?

Many of these border and medallion patterns have been used in quilts, both antique and modern, pictured previously in this series. Dozens of their block patterns have already been given in the *Baltimore Beauties* series. Several of the quilts pictured will be featured for the first time, along with some or all of their block patterns in *Volume III*. If two or more of their block patterns will appear in *Volume III*, this is noted in the quilt's Color Section caption.

The Medallions and Victorian Sentiment

There are two dramatic patterns in this book for enlarged center medallion designs. The first medallion is one of my favorites because of its design; it is graphic, strong, and simple. Pattern #11, The "Bowl of Flowers in a Rose Wreath" is, in my experience, a one-of-a-kind center medallion. The second (Pattern #12) combines the famous Updegraf feather-wreathed medallion border with a gold laid-work Album enclosed in a lyre wreath of roses. In the original (Quilt #8 in *Baltimore Beauties, Volume II),* the center had the traditional basket, bird, and book motif whose pattern is in my first book, *Spoken Without a Word.* Counting the "Basket, Bird, and Book" pattern in *Spoken Without a Word* as number three, there are five medallion center patterns in my Album books. The fourth one is the repeat-block "Peony Center" in *Volume I's* pattern companion, *Baltimore Album Quilts.* And the fifth is the charming "Inscribed Rose Wreath" presented on the pattern pull-out sheet in *Dimensional Appliqué.*

We can extrapolate a simple Album medallion design formula from the two medallions pictured in the Color

Section. With this, one can design one's own medallion center. Such an enlarged center block formula might read:

In the Outer Position: A border, or plain cloth, or flower sprigged corners

In the Middle Position: A wreath frame (variable wreath shapes)

In the Inner Position: A center motif (basket, bird, and book; bowl of flowers; building; silhouette portrait; scene; or a calligraphed inscription)

In Pattern #11, for example, there is no medallion border, just open corners. In some ornate medallion centers, a white silk rose pins each corner, but nothing more. In Pattern #12 a formal straight-spined feather plume ties the central medallion to the undulating feather plume of the original quilt's border (Pattern #6). As for the wreath frames, a basic circle-shaped wreath and a lyre-shaped wreath are pictured. From this we understand that we could have a heart-shaped wreath, or any of the numerous and wonderful wreath shapes that populate the Album Quilts. Like Pattern #11, the simple rose/leaf repeat on a circular stem ties the medallion to the border's dramatic rose/leaf repeat on a straight stem (Pattern #10). In the Album mood, the center motifs of a book — an Album of friendship perhaps, or the Album of one's life — and a bowl of sweet-scented flowers edged by birds, symbols of the soul, seem quietly evocative as thematic quilt motifs. Before we proceed to the drawn patterns themselves, let's set the appliqué scene by considering what thoughts this book's border designs may symbolize.

BORDER THEMES

Design a Baltimore Album Quilt! gives a quick pictorial overview of Album Quilt border motifs. Skimming those pictures, one sees that the border motifs used are confined to a relatively limited number of themes, presented in a variety of ways. The ten border patterns in this book contain these themes:

■ The Classic Revival Themes (Pattern #8) are:

1. Laurel Garland, symbolizing Victory, Courage, Reknown.

2. The Palmetto or Shell Motif, a design taken from atop the Parthenon's tiles, symbolizes the classic ideals of balance and beauty. There was also a moral attribute to

neo-classicism. "Roman morality," as it was called, was admired and to be emulated.

3. The Acanthus, whose scrolling leaves frame the border dates and initials, reaches back even beyond ancient Greece and Rome to ancient Egypt and the idealized Temple of Solomon. In the "Language of the Flowers," Acanthus took on the meaning, "appreciative of the fine arts." Neo-Classicism and Neo-Romanism were strong cultural influences whose themes thread the mid-19th-century Baltimore-style Album Quilts.

■ Fruits and Flowers, Stems and Vines (Patterns #1, 3, 7, 8, 9, and 10):

Vines are conduits of life. The vineyard symbolizes the church, the source of spiritual life. Vines of Roses symbolize love, emphasize connectedness and the protective power of love. It's interesting to note that the hearts and angels, which adorn two of these border patterns, are modern additions, tucked into traditional designs by Kathie Campbell and me. And what would a modern quiltmaker see in these symbols? Love, beneficence, and protectiveness, perhaps.

■ Medallion Centers (Patterns #11 and 12):

Both of the patterns given here are Containers of Blessings. The Urn symbolized to Masons and Odd Fellows the sweet soul (the incense) ascending heavenward, and since ancient times, was regarded as the Vessel of Life. The Book (inscribed Bible, Hymns, Sacred Hymns, The Album, or Lady's Album) stands for the Odd Fellows, in particular, for truth and the spiritual life.

■ Connectors: Ribbons, Tassels, Feather Plumes, Swags (hammocks or canopies):

Other than the feather plumes, these motifs go back to antiquity and enjoyed popular revival in the Renaissance. In the Albums, these seem all to be connectors, tying the lives represented in the quilt together in friendship and community. "Succor the widow and orphan" went the watchword of the day, and even ribbons reinforced one's duty, one to another. Birds have long been border motifs, and hence, perhaps, they and their feathered plumes represent both Messengers and the Life of the Soul, a life well-nourished by the Album Quilts. And on that lofty note, let's go on to our border and medallion patterns!

Part Two: The Patterns

Border Pattern No. 1 – The Home-Grown Rose Border
Page 1 of 3, Left Side of Corner

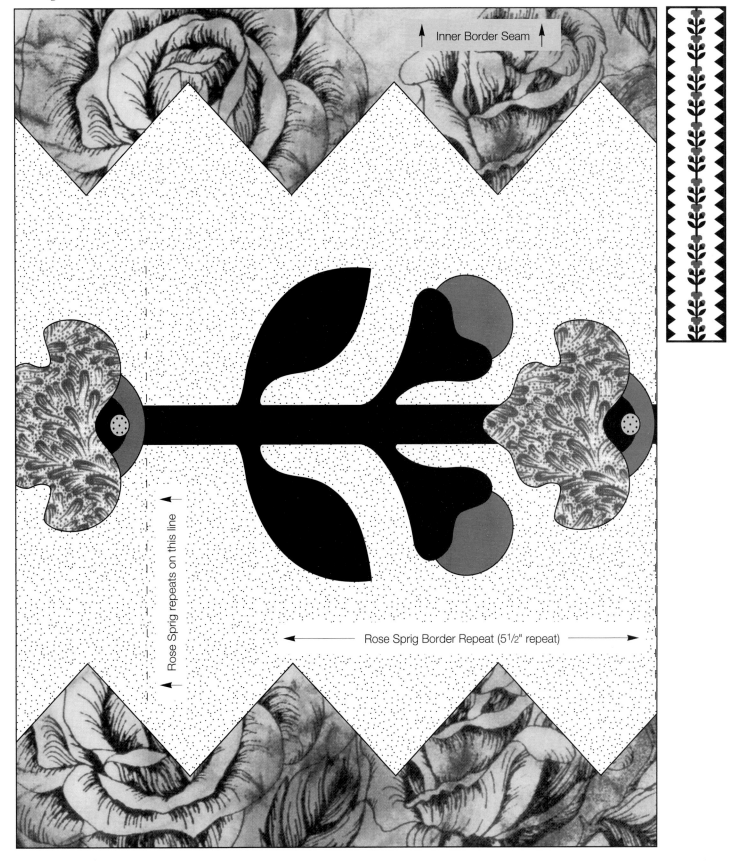

Inner Border Seam

Rose Sprig repeats on this line

Rose Sprig Border Repeat (5½" repeat)

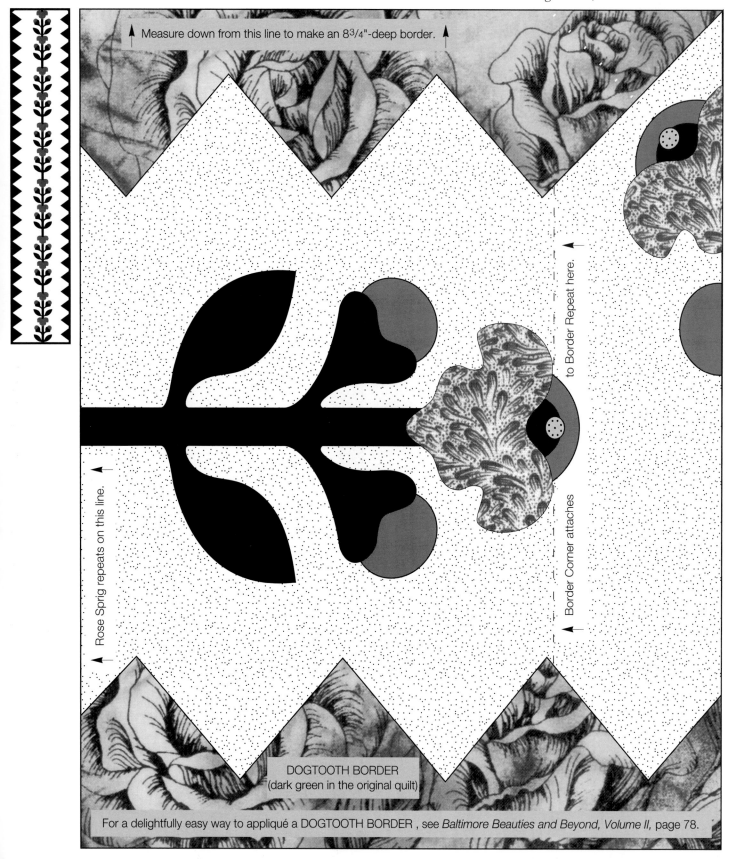

↑ Measure down from this line to make an 8³/4"-deep border. ↑

to Border Repeat here.

Rose Sprig repeats on this line.

Border Corner attaches

DOGTOOTH BORDER
(dark green in the original quilt)

For a delightfully easy way to appliqué a DOGTOOTH BORDER , see *Baltimore Beauties and Beyond, Volume II*, page 78.

Border Pattern No. 1 – The Home-Grown Rose Border
Page 3 of 3, Corner

THE HOME-GROWN
ROSE BORDER

This line bisects the border's corner

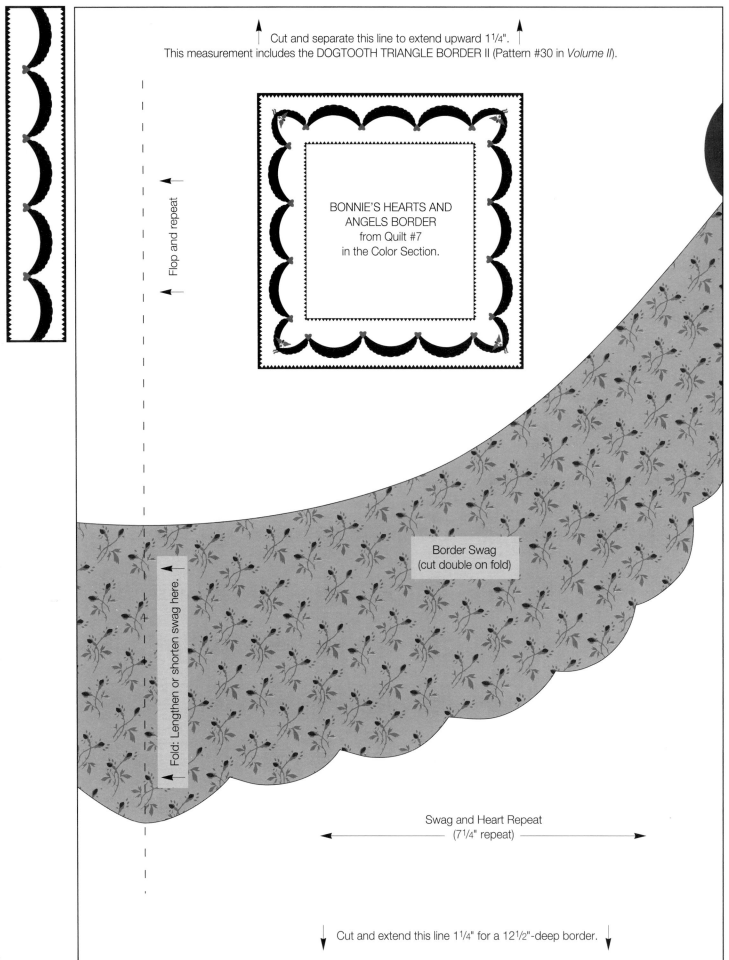

Cut and separate this line to extend upward 1¼".
This measurement includes the DOGTOOTH TRIANGLE BORDER II (Pattern #30 in *Volume II*).

Flop and repeat

BONNIE'S HEARTS AND
ANGELS BORDER
from Quilt #7
in the Color Section.

Border Swag
(cut double on fold)

Fold: Lengthen or shorten swag here.

Swag and Heart Repeat
(7¼" repeat)

Cut and extend this line 1¼" for a 12½"-deep border.

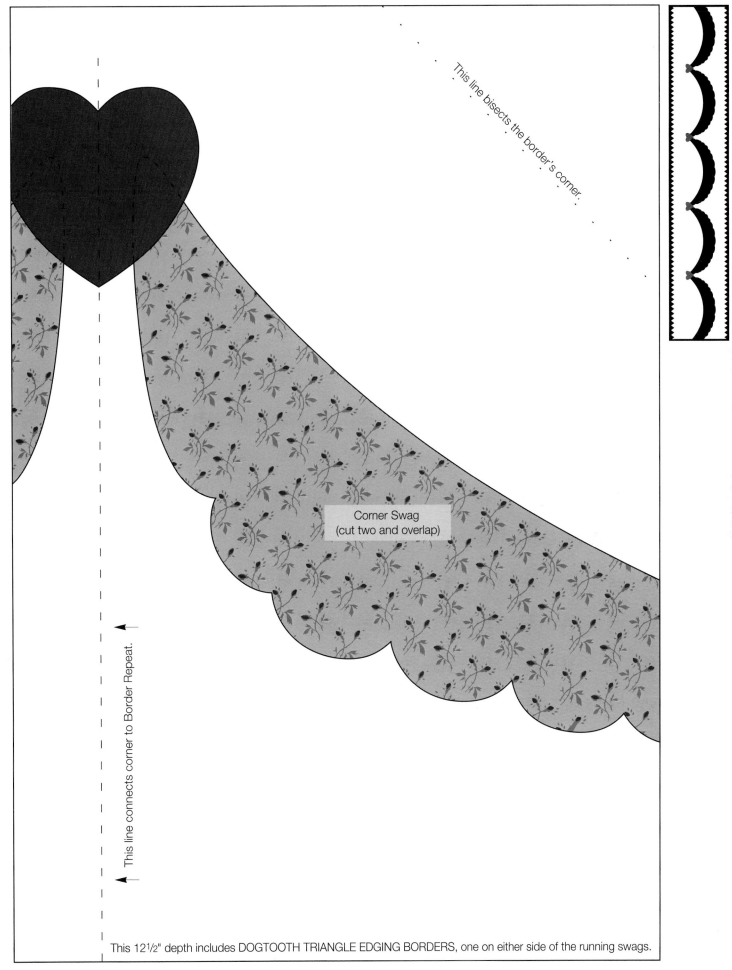

This line bisects the border's corner.

Corner Swag
(cut two and overlap)

This line connects corner to Border Repeat.

This 12½" depth includes DOGTOOTH TRIANGLE EDGING BORDERS, one on either side of the running swags.

Using this basic pattern,
Kathie made each of the angels
in the quilt's four corners
slightly different.

This line bisects the border's corner.

Pattern Note:

The original ROSE OF SHARON BORDER (Quilt #6 in the Color Section) is a masterpiece of stuffed, quilted, and embroidered appliqué. By hand, the wool straight-stitch embroidery must have taken a long time. With a scallop stitch for the flowers and a blanket stitch for the leaves, wool embroidery on the sewing machine gives the antique opulence in a fraction of the time. Or, you may prefer hand appliqué, unembellished with embroidery.

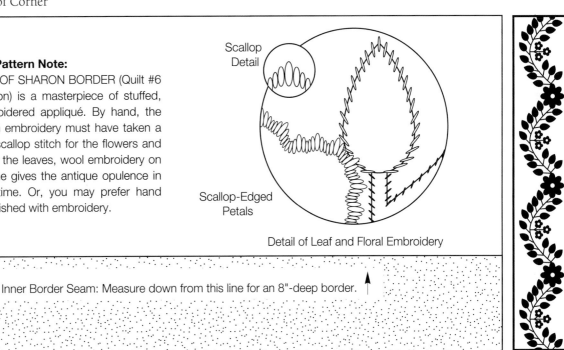

Scallop Detail

Scallop-Edged Petals

Detail of Leaf and Floral Embroidery

↑ Inner Border Seam: Measure down from this line for an 8"-deep border. ↑

↓ Extend this line ⁹/₁₆" for an 8" border. ↓

THE ROSE OF SHARON BORDER
from Quilt # 6 in the Color Section.

← 10 1/8" repeat from Large Flower Center to Large Flower Center. →

↓ Extend this line 9/16" for an 8" border. ↓

Attach border to quilt along this line.

Extend this line 9/16" for an 8" border.

This line bisects the border's corner.

Flop the Vine Stem and repeat
(Keep the leaves moving in the same direction.)

Extend this line ⁹/₁₆" for an 8" border.

Add 1" to this line for Inner Border seam line.

THE
MIRRORED-RIBBON
BORDER
from Quilt #9
in the Color Section.

Mid-line of Swag Repeat (Fold line A)

Border Swag Template's Placement Line

17" repeat from Bow Center to Bow Center.

Fold line

Add 2" to this line for 13"-deep border.

Flop and repeat.

Fold

This line connects Border Corner to Border Repeat.

Double Bow Corner's
Swag Template

Bow Template
(cut bow double on fold)

Fold line A: Cut Border Swag double on this line.

Fold line A:
For the Single Bow Corner, flop
this template and attach it at fold line
A to the Border Swag Template.

Single Bow Corner's
Swag Template

This line bisects the border's corner.

Match this line B…

…to this line B for Double Bow Corner.

Fold

Fold

↑ Inner Border Seam. ↑   Measure down from this line to make a 9"-deep border.

TASSELED-RIBBON
SWAG BORDER

Bow
(cut double on fold)

Border Swag
(cut double on fold)

Fold

Fold: Flop pattern and repeat.

6¹/₂" repeat
from center of Bow to Center of Border Swag

For the Corner: Center the Bow
(between two swags)
on the line that bisects the border's corner.

This line bisects the border's corner.

Pattern Transfer Note:

The master pattern for the left side border of this design should be the full length of the border. Flop the entire pattern for the right side of border. The layout pattern for the BERIBBONED FEATHER BORDER should be traced onto the white background fabric. It gets reverse appliquéd to a second fabric (the red fabric in Quilt #2) basted beneath. Your reverse appliquéd motifs will grow slightly as you sew. Keep the tip of each petal a soft "U-turn": one that is easy to sew by reverse appliqué. Keep a 1/4" seam allowance channel of white space between the traced petal tip and the traced spine. This white space will shrink slightly as you sew. Upon the reverse appliqué's completion, cut back the red fabric to a 3/16" seam allowance (outside of the stitch line on the underside of the border).

BERIBBONED FEATHER BORDER
from Quilt #2 in the Color Section.

Measure down from this line for an 11"-deep border.

Measure down from this line for an 11"-deep border.

(Patterns continue on page 41).

The Color Section

MANY OF THIS BOOK'S PATTERNS are here, set magnificently into quilts. In several, edging borders from *Volume II* frame this book's running border patterns. Appliquéd Paper-Cut Albums predominate here, as they do in *Volume III*. There, paper-cut quilt block patterns and how to design them star.

Quilt #1. *(Right)* BALTIMORE-STYLE ALBUM.

Made by Karen Burns. January 1990 to April 1992. 75" x 75". Block patterns from *Baltimore Beauties and Beyond, Volume I,* are enhanced by a simple set and an original-design border. This border underscores the ways in which you can vary any of this book's border patterns. (No pattern given.) (Photos: Sharon Risedorph)

Details of Quilt #2. *(Left and above)* FEATHER-WREATHED ALBUM IN A ROSE LYRE.

(Medallion Pattern #12). Made by Barbara Hahl and Yolanda Tovar. 1991. Exceptional interpretive dimensional appliqué combines here with Yolanda Tovar's *tour de force* of embroidery.

Quilt #2. *(Below)* ALBUM IN HONOR OF MOTHER.

Group quilt top made under the author's direction. 1990-1992. 81" x 81". The block patterns for this quilt are in *Dimensional Appliqué—Baskets, Blooms & Baltimore Borders.* (Photo: Jack Mathieson)

Details of Quilt #2. *(Left and below left)* BERIBBONED FEATHER BORDER.

(Border Pattern #6). These masterpiece borders were appliquéd by Sylvia Pickell and Ruth Meyers. Ruth set and edged the quilt. (Photo: S. Risedorph)

Quilt #3. *(Right)* THE NEEDLEARTIST'S ALBUM.

Group quilt under direction of the author. 1985-1992. 68" x 81". Many of the blocks in this quilt are in *Volumes I, II, III* and *Baltimore Album Quilts* of the *Baltimore Beauties* series. (Photos: J. Mathieson)

Detail of Quilt #3. *(Below)* BOWL OF FLOWERS IN A ROSE WREATH.

(Medallion Pattern #11). Exquisitely appliquéd by professional needlewoman, Joy Nichols.

Detail of Quilt #3. *(Below right)* THE STRAIGHT ROSE-VINE BORDER.

(Border Pattern #10). All borders appliquéd by Joy Nichols. They include half-circle dimensional roses.

Quilt #4. *(Below)* ODENSE ALBUM.

Group quilt made under the author's direction; professionally quilted by Mona Cumberledge. 1989-1990. 70" x 70". Most of the block patterns for this quilt are in *Baltimore Album Quilts—Historic Notes and Antique Patterns* and in *Volume II.* (Photos: S. Risedorph)

Details of Quilt #4. *(Left and below)* DANCING GRAPEVINE BORDER.

(Border Pattern #7). All four borders appliquéd by Albertine Veenstra.

Quilt #5. (*Below*) THE CLASSIC REVIVAL ALBUM.

Group quilt made under the author's direction. 1985-1991. 96" x 96". Most of this quilt's block patterns, as well as its needleartists' biographies are in *Volume III*. The border's initials, A.C.S., are those of the author's middle child, Alex Corbly Sienkiewicz, for whom the quilt was made. (Photos: S. Risedorph)

Detail of Quilt #5. (*Right and below*) PALMETTO-TIED LAUREL GARLAND BORDER.

(Border Pattern #8). Appliquéd by Albertine Veenstra and Nonna Crook.

Quilt #6. (*Below left*) BALTIMORE-STYLE ALBUM QUILT.

Mid-19th century. 100½" x 100½". Much of this quilt, including the border, is heavily stuffed and embroidered. (Photos: Adam A. Weschler & Sons)

Detail of Quilt #6. (*Below right*) ROSE OF SHARON BORDER. (Border Pattern #3).

Quilt #7. (*Left*) BONNIE'S ALBUM.

Designed and made by Kathryn Blomgren Campbell for her daughter Bonnie Elizabeth (born 3/25/77). February 1988 to December 1989. 86" x 103". Kathie inscribed an old English verse in one of the border's corners, "Four angels round my bed/ Four angels round my head/ Two to watch and one to pray/ And one to wipe my tears away." Several of the block patterns from this quilt are given in *Volume III.* (Photo: Barbara Hunt).

Quilt #8. *(Lower right)* FRIENDSHIP'S OFFERING.

Group Quilt. Made under direction of the author and Kate Fowle. 1986-1988. 115" x 115". The friends of Mary Sue Thomas Hannan who made this quilt for her are listed in *Volume I*. Its full block patterns are given in *Volume III*. (Photos: Gary E. Garrison)

Quilt #9. *(Right)* LINDSAY'S ALBUM.

Made by Kathryn Blomgren Campbell for her daughter, Lindsay Kathryn (born 8/7/74). February 1988 to December 1989. 95" x 95". This is inspired by "The Mirrored-Ribbon Border" from Quilt #2 in *Design a Baltimore Album Quilt*. To make this border, use Border Pattern #4. (Photo: B. Hunt)

Detail of Quilt #7. *(Below)* BONNIE'S HEARTS AND ANGELS BORDER CORNER. (Border Pattern #2). (Photo: B. Hunt)

Details of Quilt #8. (Border Pattern #9).

Two ORIGINAL BLOCK DESIGNS. (no pattern) Joop Smits of the Netherlands. They are good examples of the kind of blocks that can be framed by a wreath or by a paper-cut border to enlarge them into a center medallion. (Photo: J. Smits)

Quilt #10. *(Below)* CELEBRATE AMERICA.

1492-1992. Designed and made by Victoria Miller. 1992. 100" x 102". Many block patterns from the *Baltimore Beauties* series are used in this award-winning quilt. (Photos: Helen Kohler-Rickman)

Detail of Quilt #10.

Measure down from this line for an 11"-deep border.

This line bisects the border's corner.

This line bisects the border's corner.

Flop the entire pattern for the
right side of Top Border.

This line bisects the border's corner.

This border section is the same as the border on page 27.

This line bisects the border's corner.

Measure up from this line for an 11"-deep border.

This border section is the same as the border on page 45.

This line bisects the border's corner.

Flop the entire pattern for
the right side of Bottom Border.

Measure down from this line for an 11"-deep border.

Border Center

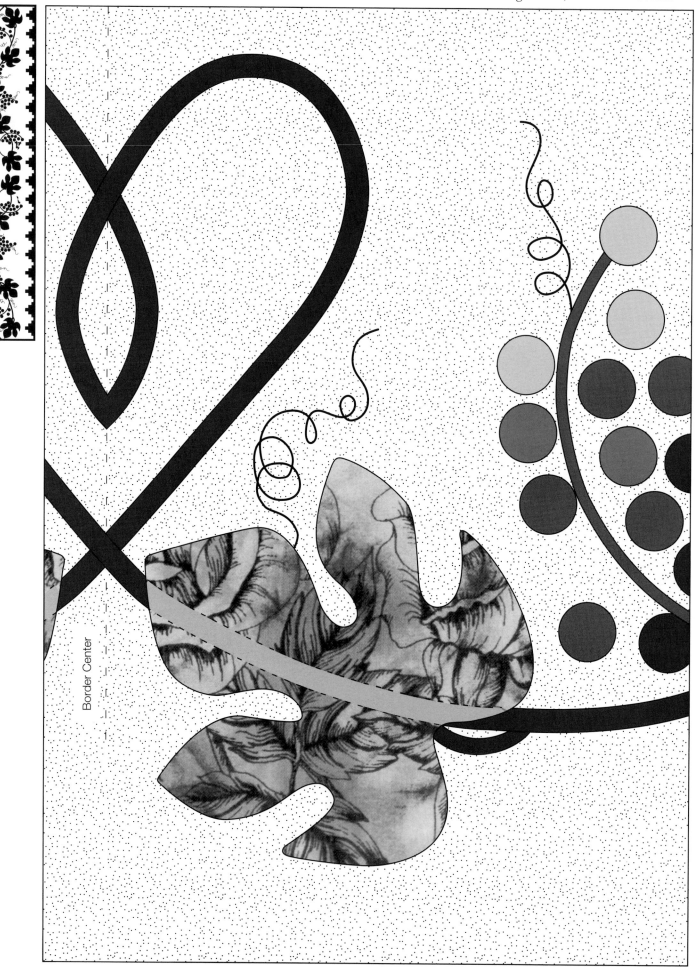

Border Center

Measure down from this line for a 12" deep border.

Measure down from this line for a 12" deep border.

Use Pattern 32, *Volume II*,
as a guide in making the
THREE-STEP EDGING BORDER
to this scale.

This line bisects the border's corner

THE DANCING
GRAPEVINE BORDER
from Quilt #4 in
the Color Section.

This is a 12"-wide border. The 12" includes the THREE-STEP EDGING BORDER. Where the grapes come close to the highest "step," make that top step just ¼" deep, as shown at A.

This line bisects the border's corner.

Bottom Border Center

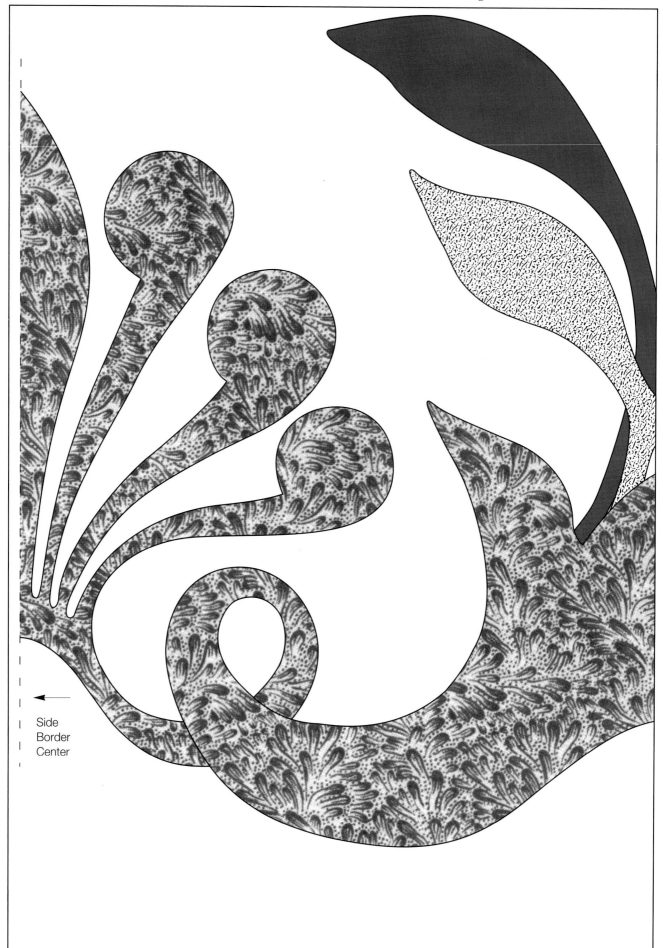

Side
Border
Center

Position the Laurel Vine so that it is centered along the middle of a 12"-wide border.

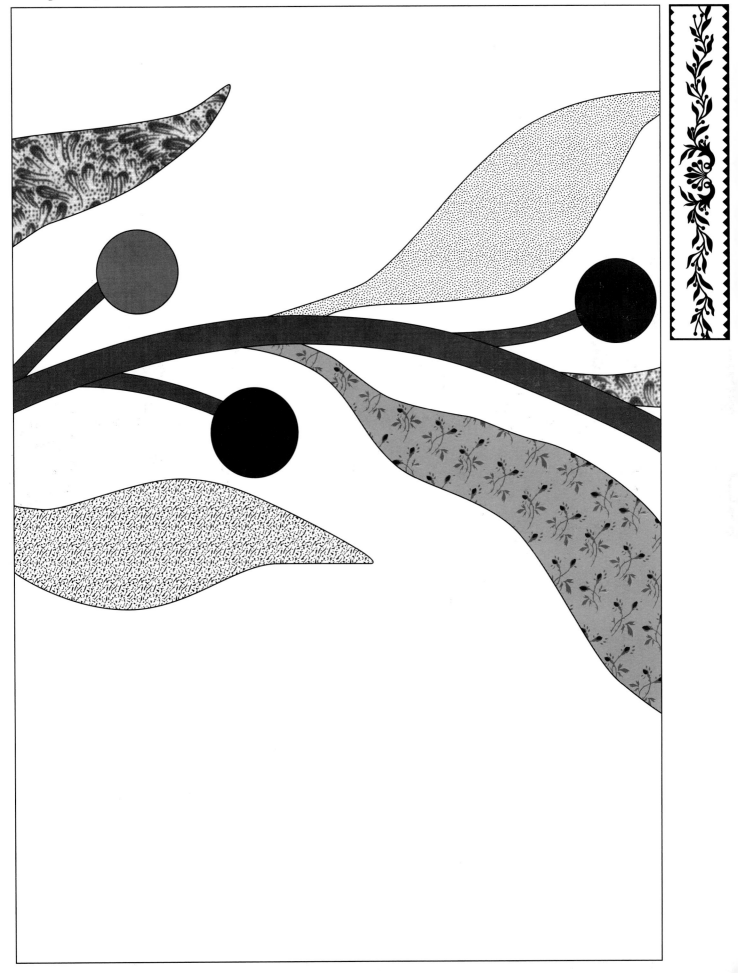

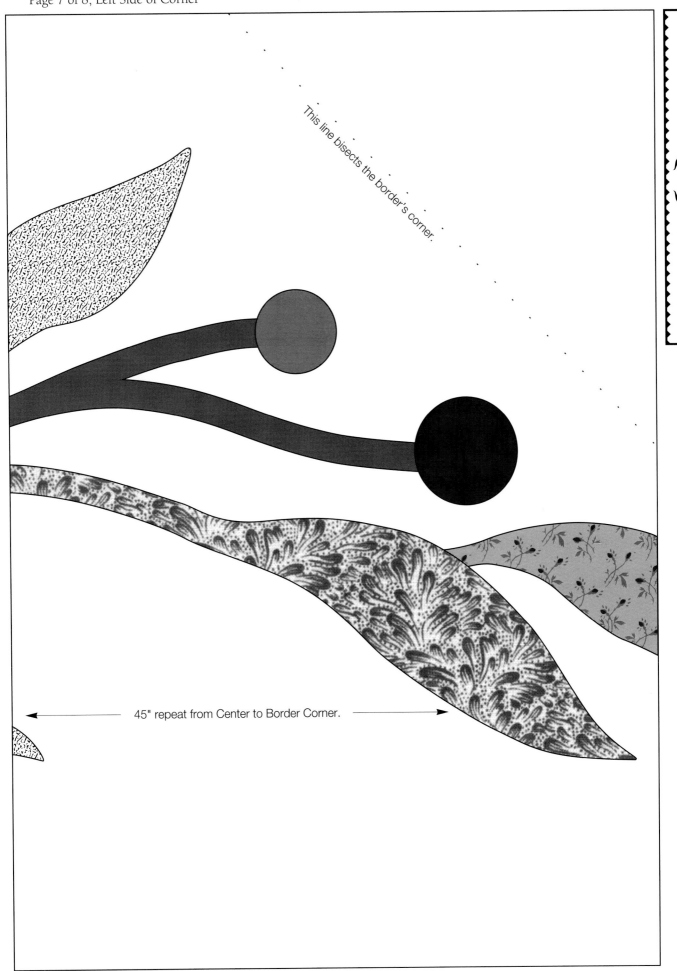

This line bisects the border's corner.

45" repeat from Center to Border Corner.

THE PALMETTO-TIED LAUREL
GARLAND BORDER
from Quilt #5 in Color Section.

1992

This line bisects the border's corner.

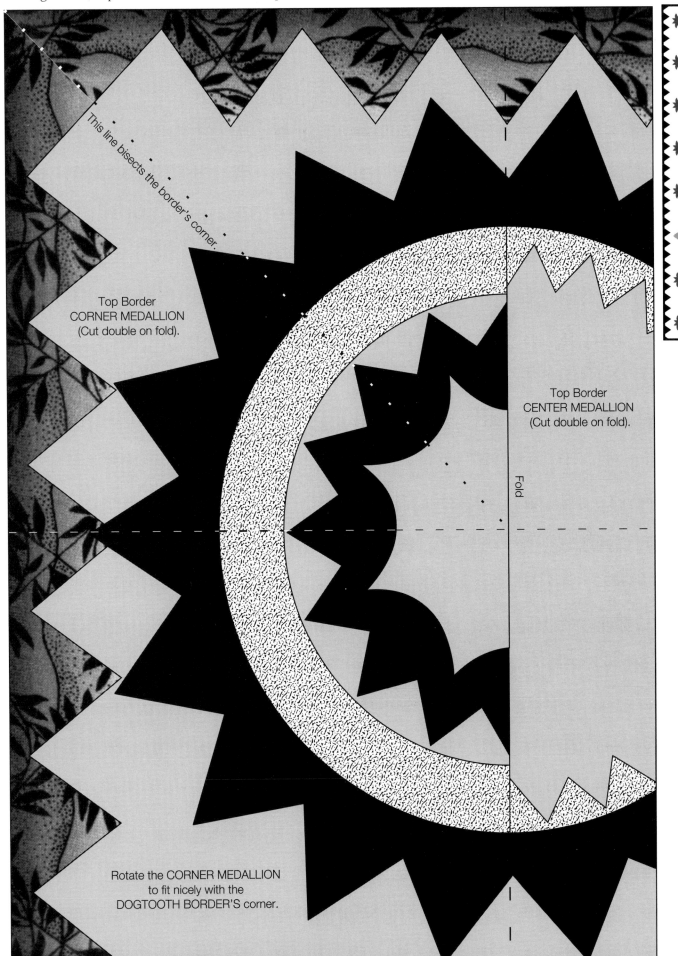

This line bisects the border's corner.

Top Border
CORNER MEDALLION
(Cut double on fold).

Top Border
CENTER MEDALLION
(Cut double on fold).

Fold

Rotate the CORNER MEDALLION
to fit nicely with the
DOGTOOTH BORDER'S corner.

Measure down from this line for an
11"-deep border.

The DOGTOOTH BORDER II comes to this line. See Pattern #30 in *Volume II.*

Measure down from this line for an 11"-deep border.

This is the Border Vine Repeat (a 6¹/₂" repeat).

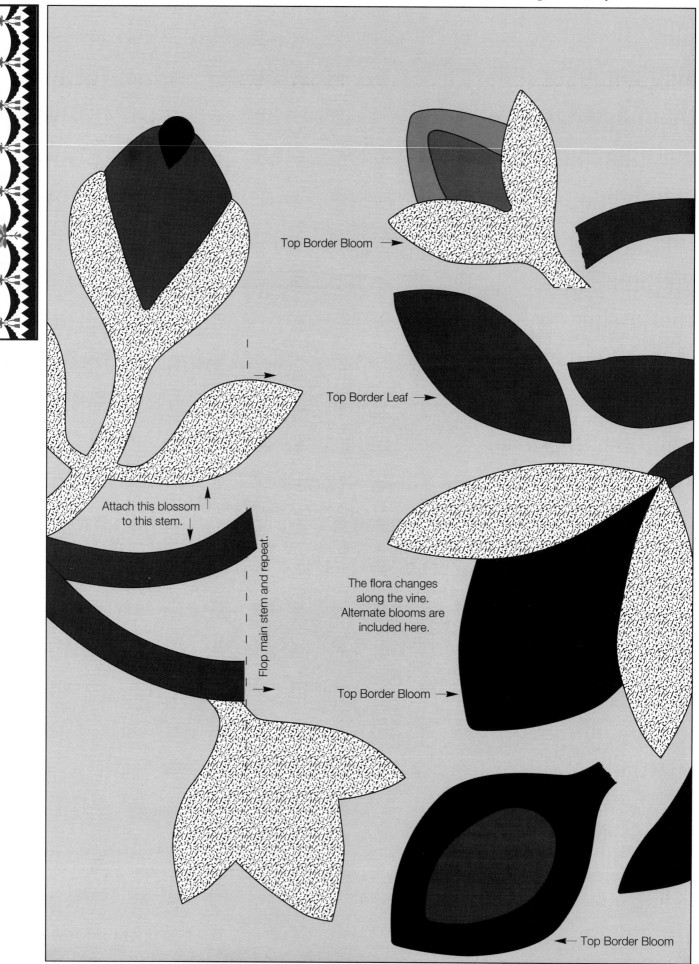

Top Border Bloom →

Top Border Leaf →

Attach this blossom
to this stem.

Flop main stem and repeat.

The flora changes
along the vine.
Alternate blooms are
included here.

Top Border Bloom →

← Top Border Bloom

Use this stem to
connect the Border
Vine to the Border
CORNER MEDALLION.

FRIENDSHIP'S
OFFERING BORDER
from Quilt #8 in the
Color Section.

← Top Border Bloom

This motif joins
the Side Border
Swag to the Border
CORNER
MEDALLIONS
at the top.

Inner border seam

Side Border Peony
(cut double on fold)

Flop and repeat Side
Border Swag on this line.

Bottom Center Border Motif (cut double on the fold)

Fold

Side Border Swag

Side Border Repeat (3¼" repeat)

Fold

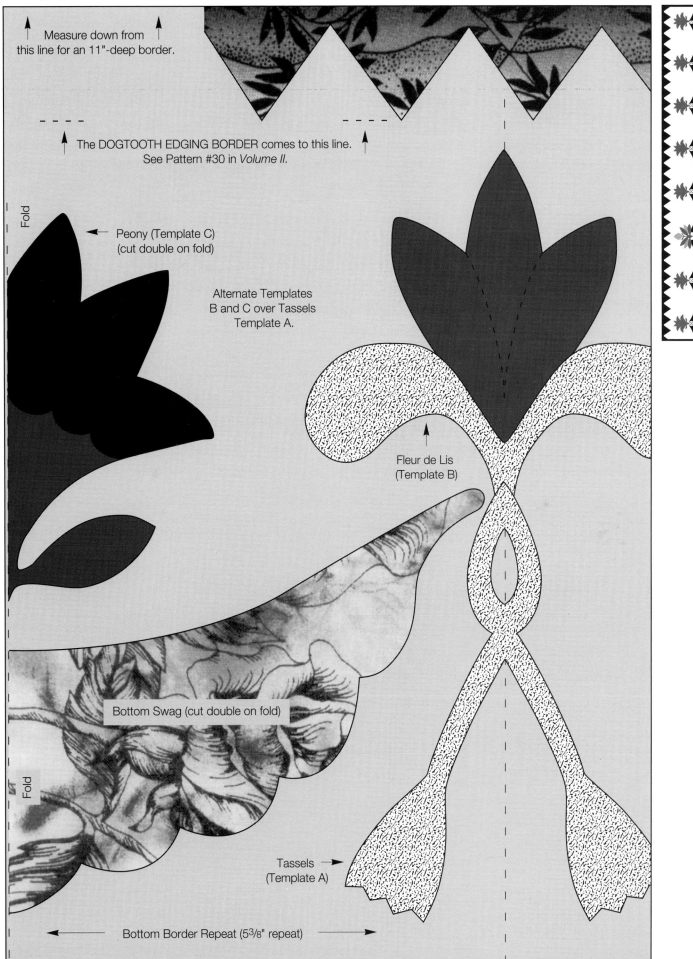

Measure down from
this line for an 11"-deep border.

The DOGTOOTH EDGING BORDER comes to this line.
See Pattern #30 in *Volume II.*

Fold

Peony (Template C)
(cut double on fold)

Alternate Templates
B and C over Tassels
Template A.

Fleur de Lis
(Template B)

Bottom Swag (cut double on fold)

Fold

Tassels
(Template A)

Bottom Border Repeat (5³/₈" repeat)

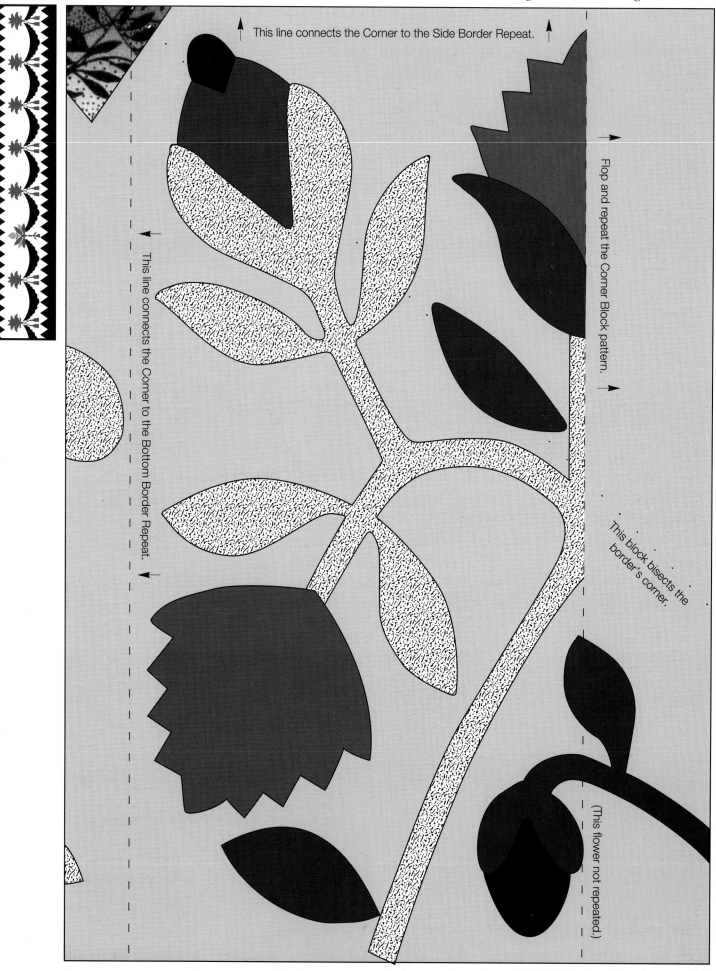

This line connects the Corner to the Side Border Repeat.

This line connects the Corner to the Bottom Border Repeat.

Flop and repeat the Corner Block pattern.

This block bisects the border's corner.

(This flower not repeated.)

Part Three: The Quiltmakers

About the Needleartists Whose Work Appears in *Appliqué 12 Borders and Medallions!* Time and talent, generously given, have made the *Baltimore Beauties* series possible. It has continued because of the enthusiastic support of needleartists who have made pattern models from kits, or interpreted patterns in cloth, or designed whole blocks and patterns themselves. Some have shared photographs of their already completed work. The enthusiasm of these ladies and their friendship have been essential to both the quilts they have helped to make and to the very existence of this series. They, each and every one, have my profound gratitude. *Note:* The brief biographies here are based on replies to my needleartist questionnaires. Biographical notes on a given needleartist tend to appear only once in the series, even though their work may appear in several volumes. Additional needleartists whose work is featured in the Color Section have biographical notes in earlier volumes and in *Volume III*.

KAREN BURNS of Pleasanton, California: Baltimore-style Album Quilt.

A quiltmaker for about three years now, this was the first big quilt Karen quilted. She began it in a year-long block-a-month class taught by a skilled and influential teacher, Nadine Thompson, at the Going to Pieces Quilt Shop in Pleasanton. Once completed, the quilt won Best of Show in the 1992 Alameda County Fair and, in 1993, took these prizes at the Marin County Fair: two Judge's Choice awards, Viewers' Choice, and second place in appliqué. Karen designed the border pattern, the cornucopia block, and an exceptional Album Quilt!

KATHRYN BLOMGREN CAMPBELL of Washington, D.C.: Bonnie's Hearts and Angels Border, Bonnie's Album, and Lindsay's Album.

Kathie became a Phi Beta Kappa with a major in Psychology after her daughters entered school. She is an avid genealogist and collector of antique needlework. Largely self-taught in quiltmaking, she and the author are neighbors, two houses apart. They have same-age daughters who are close friends, and they worked together with the Schoolhouse Quilters for several years, making raffle quilts for their children's school, Lafayette Elementary. Inspired by the concept of paper-cut quilts, Kathie began designing and making two spectacular quilts, one for each of her daughters. She shares a border pattern here, and several of her original block patterns in *Volume III*.

BARBARA A. HAHL of Boca Raton, Florida: Feather-Wreathed Album in a Rose Lyre (made with Yolanda Tovar whose needleartist biography is in *Dimensional Appliqué*).

Barbara has sewn from childhood (dolls, clothes, 4-H). Her skills expanded to include upholstery, menswear, formal dresses, and since the mid-'70s, quilting. She is an award-winning quiltmaker and teaches quiltmaking as well. Barbara has shared her love of quiltmaking as president of her guild, through the guild's annual quilt show and its sponsorship of the Smithsonian Exhibition, "Homage To Amanda," by participation in Florida's state quilt search and other community events, and by her gift to the *Baltimore Beauties* series.

VICTORIA L. MILLER of Northfield, Minnesota: Celebrate America 1492-1992.

Victoria made this elegant quilt "to commemorate the Quincentennial of America—thus, the significance of the Mariner's Compass in the border. The quilt is also meant to be a celebration of family and friends. (Four of the blocks were made by friends.) This quilt won second place (group category) at the 1992 AIQA Show, Houston, Texas."

JOOP SMITS of Bilthoven, Netherlands: Basket of Flowers and Riderless Horse.

Joop and I met at Quilt Europa '90 in Odense, Denmark. She is a well-loved international quiltmaker of remarkable talent. She teaches quiltmaking "full-time," and does her own designing. The fabrics she uses most are recycled from other things and mixed with an artist's touch. Joop and her husband spend much of their time traveling all over the world visiting their nine children. She is currently working on a Baltimore-like Album quilt into which she has put remembrances of all her children, their jobs, and their hobbies.

Appendix: Classes

*T*he following descriptions of possible quilting classes use *Appliqué 12 Borders and Medallions!* as a pattern source. Anyone who would like to teach these course formats, or organize a study group around them, has the author's and the publisher's permission to print these descriptions.

A BALTIMORE BORDERS TUTORIAL

Eight 2½-hour classes: Almost Ready for Appliqué Borders? Join this inspiring and practical seminar to explore the possibilities and start a border project. We'll cover these topics: 1. Making and tailoring a master border pattern for your quilt (one session). 2. Choosing the most suitable method for appliqué and pattern transfer. Preparing the appliqués (one session). 3. Appliquéing the border (four sessions). 4. Attaching the borders, quilting and binding options (one session), and Border Completion Celebration (one session).

Supplies: Come to the first class with your blocks, set ideas, and materials to make a master border pattern. (Review pages 66-72 in *Design a Baltimore Album Quilt!* Bring that book, and for patterns, *Baltimore Beauties, Volume II,* and *Appliqué 12 Borders and Medallions!*)

A BALTIMORE MEDALLIONS TUTORIAL

Five 2½-hour classes: Come join this lively medallion study group for both inspiration and instruction. We'll cover these topics: 1. Making a master medallion pattern tailored to your set (one session). 2. Design your own medallion or use a printed pattern? Consider your options. Pattern transfer and the appliqué preparation (one session). 3. Appliquéing the medallion center (two sessions). 4. Medallion Completion Celebration (one session).

Supplies: Come to the first class with your blocks, set ideas, and materials to make a master medallion pattern. (Review pages 66-72 in *Design a Baltimore Album Quilt!* Bring *Spoken Without a Word, Dimensional Appliqué,* and *Appliqué 12 Borders and Medallions!* for pattern selection.)

Other Books by Elly Sienkiewicz

• *Spoken Without A Word*
A Lexicon of Selected Symbols with 24 Patterns From Classic Baltimore Album Quilts (1983). Available from The Cotton Patch, 1025 Brown Avenue, Lafayette, CA 94549. ($18.95 plus $4 s/h; CA residents add 8¼% tax.)

• *Baltimore Beauties and Beyond*
Studies in Classic Album Quilt Appliqué, Volume I (1989).

• *Baltimore Album Quilts, Historic Notes and Antique Patterns*
A Pattern Companion to Baltimore Beauties and Beyond, Studies in Classic Album Quilt Appliqué, Volume I (1990).

• *Baltimore Beauties and Beyond*
Studies in Classic Album Quilt Appliqué, Volume II (1991).

• *Appliqué 12 Easy Ways!*
Charming Quilts, Giftable Projects, and Timeless Techniques (1991).

• *Design a Baltimore Album Quilt!*
A Teach-Yourself Course in Sets and Borders
A Design Companion to Baltimore Beauties and Beyond, Studies in Classic Album Quilt Appliqué, Volume II (1992).

• *Dimensional Appliqué, Baskets, Blooms, and Baltimore Borders*
A Pattern Companion to Baltimore Beauties and Beyond, Studies in Classic Album Quilt Appliqué, Volume II (1993).

• *Baltimore Album Revival!*
Historic Quilts in the Making. Catalog of the 1994 C&T Baltimore Album Revival Quilt Show and Contest (1994).

• *Baltimore Beauties and Beyond*
Studies in Classic Album Quilt Appliqué, Volume III (1995).

For these and other fine books, write or call:
C&T Publishing, 5021 Blum Road #1, Martinez, CA 94553.
Telephone: 1-800-284-1114.